DO YOU KNOW ?

Level 1

TALL TOWERS

Written by Hannah Fish
Series Editor: Nick Coates

LADYBIRD BOOKS

UK | USA | Canada | Ireland | Australia
India | New Zealand | South Africa

Ladybird Books Ltd is part of the Penguin Random House group of companies
whose addresses can be found at global.penguinrandomhouse.com.
www.penguin.co.uk   www.puffin.co.uk   www.ladybird.co.uk

Penguin
Random House
UK

First published 2021
001

Text copyright © Ladybird Books Ltd, 2021
Illustrations by Dynamo Limited
Illustrations copyright © Ladybird Books Ltd, 2021

Printed in China

The authorized representative in the EEA is Penguin Random House Ireland,
Morrison Chambers, 32 Nassau Street, Dublin D02 YH68

A CIP catalogue record for this book is available from the British Library

ISBN: 978-0-241-50338-6

All correspondence to:
Ladybird Books
Penguin Random House Children's
One Embassy Gardens, 8 Viaduct Gardens, London SW11 7BW

MIX
Paper from
responsible sources
FSC® C018179

Contents

New words

build
(verb)

city

different

difficult

heavy

metal

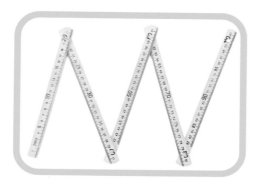

metre

shape
(noun)

soft

strong

tall

work
(verb)

What is a tower?

A tower is a **tall** building. Towers have lots of floors.

People **work** in these towers.

Petronas Towers, Malaysia

People live in this tower. It has 85 floors!

432 Park Avenue, USA

85 floors

Oriental Pearl Tower, China

THINK!

Do you live in a tower?

How tall are towers?

Some towers are very tall.
The Tokyo Skytree is 634 **metres** tall.

At night this tower
is blue, purple
or orange!

The Skytree, Japan

634 metres

This tower is very tall, too. It is 632 metres tall.

Shanghai Tower, China

632 metres

This tower is 601 metres tall.

The Makkah Royal Clock Tower, Saudi Arabia

601 metres

FIND OUT!

Use books or the internet to find out how many floors does the Shanghai Tower have?

Are some towers old?

Some towers are very old.
These towers are 5,000
years old. You can see these
old towers today.

Vainakh Towers,
Chechen Republic, Russia

These three pagodas are very old, too. They are 1,100 years old!

Three Pagodas, China

FIND OUT!

Use books or the internet to find out about old towers in your country.

Does the Tower of Pisa lean?

Look at the Tower of Pisa. It is leaning. The walls are **heavy** . . . and the floor is **soft**.

The Leaning Tower of Pisa, Italy

walls

The Tower of London has **strong** walls.

The Tower of London, England

📖 **FIND OUT!**

Use books or the internet.
Why did the Tower of London need strong walls?

13

What is Jenney's story?

It is 1884. William Le Baron Jenney makes buildings.

One day, Jenney is at home. He sees a heavy book on a little birdcage. The birdcage is very strong. It has a **metal** frame. Jenney **builds** a tower with a metal frame. His tower is strong, too!

Today, buildings have metal frames.

William Le Baron Jenney

birdcage

metal frame

Jenney's Home
Insurance Building, USA

THINK!

Why is the birdcage design used for big buildings?

What is a skyscraper?

A skyscraper is a very tall tower. The Chrysler Building is a beautiful skyscraper.

The Chrysler Building has 3,862 windows.

The Chrysler Building, USA

Today, many **cities** have skyscrapers.

Hong Kong, China

PROJECT

Think of your own skyscraper. Now, draw a picture of your skyscraper.

What is the Burj Khalifa?

The Burj Khalifa is a very tall skyscraper. It is 830 metres tall!

There is a swimming pool on floor 76!

swimming pool

Burj Khalifa, UAE

floor 148

There is a big window on floor 148. You can see the city!

LOOK!

Look at the pages.

What different things can you see from floor 148 of the Burj Khalifa?

Who cleans the windows of the Burj Khalifa?

The Burj Khalifa has lots of windows. Cleaning the windows is **difficult**. Look at this person. They are above the clouds!

The Burj Khalifa has 24,348 windows!

clouds

WATCH!

Watch the video (see page 32).
Why is this a difficult job?

What shape are towers?

There are many **different shapes** of towers.

This tower is a triangle shape.

Eiffel Tower, France

triangle

This building is a triangle shape, too.

The Flatiron Building, USA

rectangle

This tower has lots of rectangles.

The Cube, Lebanon

PROJECT

Work with a friend.
Look at the towers in this book.
Draw a tower using a different shape.

This tower has a ride on it. It is a hand shape.

This tower is a T shape. You can see the Niagara Falls from here.

The Stratosphere Tower, USA

LOOK!

Look at pages 22–25.
Which tower is your favourite? Why?

Which towers help people?

People live and work in towers. Towers can help people, too. Lighthouses help boats at night.

Beachy Head Lighthouse, England

This tower tells people the time.

The Zytglogge Tower, Switzerland

This tower gives people radio and television.

The Berlin TV Tower, Germany

▶ WATCH!

Watch the video (see page 32).
How do lighthouses help boats?

Can towers be green?

Some new towers can help a city. These towers have got lots of trees and green plants.

plants

Garden of Eden, Singapore

iconic hotel building, Singapore

plants

Look at these green towers.
They are very different!

Bosco Verticale, Italy

PROJECT

Think about a new green tower.
Make a poster with labels!

Quiz

Choose the correct answers.

1 A tower is a . . .
   a tall building.
   b small building.

2 The Vainakh
Towers are . . .
   a old towers.
   b new towers.

3 Building a tower is . . .
   a not difficult.
   b difficult.

4 The Burj Khalifa is . . .
  a 380 metres tall.
  b 830 metres tall.

5 Lighthouses help . . .
  a cars at night.
  b boats at night.

DO YOU KNOW?

Visit **www.ladybirdeducation.co.uk** for
FREE **DO YOU KNOW?** teaching resources.

- video clips with simplified voiceover and subtitles
- video and comprehension activities
- class projects and lesson plans
- audio recording of every book
- digital version of every book
- full answer keys

To access video clips, audio tracks and digital books:

1 Go to **www.ladybirdeducation.co.uk**
2 Click 'Unlock book'
3 Enter the code below

LnHx9cQxWv

Stay safe online! Some of the DO YOU KNOW? activities ask children to do extra research online. Remember:

- ensure an adult is supervising;
- use established search engines such as Google or Kiddle;
- children should never share personal details, such as name, home or school address, telephone number or photos.